TABLE OF CONTENTS   PAGE

INTRODUCTION

The first part of the book deals with the history of human rights and the key legal milestones behind some of the world's finest legal systems. The second and the final parts of the book explain some technical legal terms, phrases and the meaning of some Latin words pertaining to the field of law.

In brief, this little book is an invaluable guide to everyone who wants to know something about the law. It will prove an indispensable aid to all.

My appreciation goes to God Almighty for giving me the required strength during the time of writing. My special gratitude also goes to my children, the entire family, my 'Brethren' and the general reading public.

CHAPTER 1

A BRIEF HISTORY OF HUMAN RIGHTS AND THE LAW

In 539 B.C., the armies of Cyrus the Great, the first king of ancient Persia, conquered the city of Babylon. After his conquest, he freed all the slaves, and declared that all people had the right to choose their own religion, and established racial equality. These and other decrees were recorded on a baked-clay cylinder in the Akkadian language with cuneiform script.

Known today as the Cyrus Cylinder, this ancient record has now been recognised as the world's first charter of human rights. It is translated into all six official languages of the United Nations and its provisions parallel the first four Articles of the Universal Declaration of Human Rights.

The Spread of Human Rights

From Babylon, the idea of human rights spread quickly to India, Greece and eventually Rome. Then the concept of "natural law" arose, in observation of the fact that people tended to follow certain unwritten laws in the course of life, and Roman law was based on rational ideas derived from the nature of things.

Documents asserting individual rights, such as the *Magna Carta (1215),* the *Petition of Right* (1628), the US Constitution (1787), the French *Declaration of the Rights of Man* *and of the* Citizen (1789), and the *US Bill of Rights (1791)* are the written precursors to many of today's human rights documents.

The Magna Carta (1215) of England

The Magna Carta, or "Great Charter," was arguably the most significant early influence on the extensive historical process that led to the rule of constitutional law today in the English-speaking world.

In 1215, after King John of England violated a number of ancient laws and customs by which England had been governed, his subjects forced him to sign the Magna Carta, which enumerates what later came to be thought of as human rights. Among them was the right of the church to be free from governmental interference, the rights of all free citizens to own and inherit property and to be protected from excessive taxes. It established the right of widows who owned property to choose not to remarry, and established principles of due process and equality before the law. It also contained provisions forbidding bribery and official misconduct.

Widely viewed as one of the most important legal documents in the development of modern democracy, the Magna Carta was a crucial turning point in the struggle to establish freedom.

Petition of Right (1628)

The next recorded milestone in the development of human rights was the Petition of Right, produced in 1628 by the English Parliament and sent to Charles I as a statement of civil liberties. Refusal by Parliament to finance the king's unpopular foreign policy had caused his government to exact forced loans and to quarter troops in subjects' houses as an economy measure. Arbitrary arrest and imprisonment for opposing these policies had produced in Parliament a violent hostility to Charles and to George Villiers, the Duke of Buckingham. The Petition of Right, initiated by Sir Edward Coke, was based upon earlier statutes and charters and asserted four principles: (1) No taxes may be levied without consent of Parliament, (2) No subject may be imprisoned without cause shown (reaffirmation of the right of habeas corpus), (3) No soldiers may be quartered upon the citizenry, and (4) Martial law may not be used in time of peace.

United States Declaration of Independence (1776)

On July 4, 1776, the United States Congress approved the Declaration of Independence. Its primary author, Thomas Jefferson, wrote the Declaration as a formal explanation of why Congress had voted on July 2 to declare independence from Great Britain, more than a year after the outbreak of the American Revolutionary War, and as a statement announcing that the thirteen American Colonies were no longer a part of the British Empire. Congress issued the Declaration of Independence in several forms. It was initially published as a printed broadsheet that was widely distributed and read to the public.

Philosophically, the Declaration stressed two themes: individual rights and the right of revolution. These ideas became widely held by Americans and spread internationally as well, influencing in particular the French Revolution.

The Constitution of the United States of America (1787) and Bill of Rights (1791)

Written during the summer of 1787 in Philadelphia, the Constitution of the United States of America is the fundamental law of the US federal system of government and the landmark document of the Western world. It is the oldest written national constitution in use and defines the principal organs of government and their jurisdictions and the basic rights of citizens.

The first ten amendments to the Constitution—the Bill of Rights—came into effect on December 15, 1791, limiting the powers of the federal government of the United States and protecting the rights of all citizens, residents and visitors in American territory.

The Bill of Rights protects freedom of speech, freedom of religion, the right to keep and bear arms, the freedom of assembly and the freedom to petition. It also prohibits unreasonable search and seizure, cruel and unusual punishment and compelled self-incrimination. Among the legal protections it affords, the Bill of Rights prohibits Congress from making any law respecting establishment of religion and prohibits the federal government from depriving any person of life, liberty or property without due process of law. In federal criminal cases it requires indictment by a grand jury for any capital offense, or infamous crime, guarantees a speedy public trial with an impartial jury in the district in which the crime occurred, and prohibits double jeopardy.

Declaration of the Rights of Man and of the Citizen (1789)

In 1789 the people of France brought about the abolishment of the absolute monarchy and set the stage for the establishment of the first French Republic. Just six weeks after the storming of the Bastille, and barely three weeks after the abolition of feudalism, the Declaration of the Rights of Man and of the Citizen (French: La Déclaration des Droits de l'Homme et du Citoyen) was adopted by the National Constituent Assembly as the first step toward writing a constitution for the Republic of France.

The Declaration proclaims that all citizens are to be guaranteed the rights of "liberty, property, security, and resistance to oppression." It argues that the need for law derives from the fact that

"...the exercise of the natural rights of each man has only those borders which assure other members of the society the enjoyment of these same rights." Thus, the Declaration sees law as an "expression of the general will, "intended to promote this equality of rights and to forbid "only actions harmful to the society."

The First Geneva Convention (1864)

In 1864, sixteen European countries and several American states attended a conference in Geneva, at the invitation of the Swiss Federal Council, on the initiative of the Geneva Committee. The diplomatic conference was held for the purpose of adopting a convention for the treatment of wounded soldiers in combat.

The main principles laid down in the Convention and maintained by the later Geneva Conventions provided for the obligation to extend care without discrimination to wounded and sick military personnel and respect for and marking of medical personnel transports and equipment with the distinctive sign of the red cross on a white background.

World War II had ranged from 1939 to 1945, and as the end drew near, cities throughout Europe and Asia lay in smouldering ruins. Millions of people were dead; millions more were homeless or starving. Russian forces were closing in on the remnants of German resistance in Germany's bombed-out capital of Berlin. In the Pacific, US Marines were still battling entrenched Japanese forces on such islands as Okinawa.

In April 1945, delegates from fifty countries met in San Francisco full of optimism and hope. The goal of the United Nations Conference on International Organisation was to fashion an international body to promote peace and prevent future wars. The ideals of the organisation were stated in the preamble to its proposed charter: "We the peoples of the United Nations are determined to save succeeding generations from the scourge of war, which twice in our lifetime has brought untold sorrow to mankind."

The Charter of the new United Nations organization went into effect on October 24, 1945, a date that is celebrated each year as United Nations Day.

The Universal Declaration of Human Rights (1948)

By 1948, the United Nations' new Human Rights Commission had captured the world's attention. Under the dynamic chairmanship of Eleanor Roosevelt—President Franklin Roosevelt's widow, a human rights champion in her right and the United States delegate to the UN—the Commission set out to draft the document that became the Universal Declaration of Human Rights. Roosevelt, credited with its inspiration, referred to the Declaration as the international Magna Carta for all mankind. It was adopted by the United Nations on December 10, 1948.

In its preamble and in Article 1, the Declaration unequivocally proclaims the inherent rights of all human beings: "Disregard and contempt for human rights have resulted in barbarous acts which have outraged the conscience of mankind, and the advent of a world in which human beings shall enjoy freedom of speech and belief and freedom from fear and want has been proclaimed as the highest aspiration of the common people...All human beings are born free and equal in dignity and rights."

The Member States of the United Nations pledged to work together to promote the thirty Articles of human rights that, for the first time in history, had been assembled and codified into a single document. In consequence, many of these rights, in various forms, are today part of the constitutional laws of democratic nations.

The United Nation and Human Rights

On October 24, 1945, in the aftermath of World War II, the United Nations came into being as an intergovernmental organization, with the purpose of saving future generations from the devastation of international conflict.

The Charter of the United Nations established six principal bodies, including the General Assembly, the Security Council, the International Court of Justice, and in relation to human rights, an Economic and Social Council (ECOSOC).

The UN Charter empowered ECOSOC to establish "commissions in economic and social fields and for the promotion of human rights...." One of these was the United Nations Human Rights Commission, which, under the chairmanship of Eleanor Roosevelt, saw to the creation of the Universal Declaration of Human Rights.

The Declaration was drafted by representatives of all regions of the world and encompassed all legal traditions. Formally adopted by the United Nations on December 10, 1948, it is the most universal human rights document in existence, delineating the thirty fundamental rights that form the basis for a democratic society.

Following this historic act, the Assembly called upon all Member Countries to publicize the text of the Declaration and "to cause it to be disseminated, displayed, read and expounded principally in schools and other educational institutions, without distinction based on the political status of countries or territories."

Today, the Declaration is a living document that has been accepted as a contract between a government and its people throughout the world. According to the Guinness Book of World Records, it is the most translated document in the world.

CHAPTER 2

The origin of Common Law and Equity

The term 'common law' literally means rules of law founded in decided cases which is common to a particular locality or trade and also common to the whole country.

Common law was developed in England after 1066 when the Normans conquered the country led by William of Orange. After the conquest, the Normans discovered that England had no central legal system.

They also found that each part of England had its own local customs which they applied in its own court. So the Normans capitalised on this decentralised legal system and set the process by which the contents of law and its administration in court became common to the whole England.

The King's early judges adopted the best local customs they discovered in one particular area and then applied it to other parts of the country. This practice by the early judges brought about what is known today as the 'doctrine of precedent' in the study of law. The operation of precedent itself depends upon what has previously been decided.

Equity

Equity refers to a body of rules which originally meant fairness and justice. It also provides a different remedies and rights other than those provided by common law.

Equitable remedies include; injunction and specific performance. An injunction can take the form of 'mandatory', which is a court order to perform an act, for instance, an order perform one's obligation owed to another party in an agreement.

Injunction can also take the form of 'prohibition', which is an order giving by the court to person or an organisation not to do something, for instance, an order to stop building on someone's land or to stop an activity that will breach a contract/ agreement.

CHAPTER 3

The role of law in society

A lot of people view law in many different ways. Some think of the police and the criminal law, while others think of any rules governing day-to-day behaviour in order to bring sanity in society. Each perception is partially correct. To understand law and an established legal system, one must understand the nature of the underlying society.

Law is actually a reflection of the people, organisations and values it simultaneously serves and controls or put differently, they are formalised rules for regulating the behaviour of individuals and organisations in society. The dynamic nature of any legal system is to survive and effectively guide, and must draw from the past, reflect the present, and pave the way for the future.

One of the basic functions of law in society is to set minimum standards of behaviour which everyone in that society must observe. For instance, the law always sets out the kind of conduct which people must not engage in, such as theft, rape, murder, drink-driving, trespass etc. The law prohibits activities that can cause harm to others if allowed.

Another basic function of law is to provide a framework within which individuals and organisations can conduct their affairs with confidence and a high degree of certainty. The law in this sense may be regarded as the State's official 'stamp of authority' because apart from law, other informal rules through religion, morality, cultural norms and codes of etiquette or manners can all play a vital role in regulating behaviour in society.

CHAPTER 4

Classification of Law

Law may be classified in various ways but the two major categories of law are criminal or civil law. For the purposes of this book, we will discuss the different purposes these two areas of law serve.

Criminal law

Criminal law concerns the punishment of acts which can be seen as offending against a person or society as a whole. By means of criminal law most states regulate the conduct of individuals. Where the conduct is such as to represent a threat to the peace and well-being of the rest of society criminal law helps to impose sanctions in an attempt to supress it.

Criminal sanctions or punishments usually take the forms of imprisonment, fines, or non-custodial sanctions such as community services.

In criminal cases, the accused person is always presumed to be innocent until proven guilty. This means that the prosecution has to prove beyond reasonable doubt that the accused person is guilty. This is known as the standard of proof and it is a very high standard, which goes beyond the court just considering if it seems likely or probable that the accused is guilty.

Criminal cases are normally brought by the State through its agents called prosecutors e.g. a case against Adam will be referred to as the State versus Adam *(State v Adam)* in criminal proceedings. If Sam is acquitted, he cannot be prosecuted again for the same offence on the same evidence unless new evidence emerged against him. If Sam is convicted, he might lose some of his rights and his liberty.

Criminal law sanctions are normally imposed for the following variety of reasons which include; protection of society, reformation of offenders, recompensing on of victims and the provision of deterrence.

Prosecution of criminal offence

When a criminal offence has been committed, the normal procedure is for the police to be informed. If the police suspect a certain person of having committed the crime, they charge them and then pass the case to the State's

Prosecution Service (SPS). The SPS decides whether to prosecute and what charges to bring. The accused will appear before a Magistrate's Court.

Either his case will be heard by the Magistrate (summary trial) or he will be committed for trial in another court (trial on indictment). Some offences can be tried 'either way', i.e. summarily or on indictment depending on the choice of the defendant. If the SPS declines to act, it is still possible to bring a private prosecution.

Civil law

Civil law concerns the resolution of disputes, enforcing obligations and the payment of compensation, but not punishment (unlike criminal law), between individuals or groups of individuals. Civil cases are initiated by an aggrieved party (plaintiff / claimant), who takes legal proceedings against (sues) another party (defendant). The role of the state in civil law is to provide the means by which these disputes can be resolved.

Civil law is actually about legal obligations and it is in the interest of everyone in society that these obligations be fulfilled or if not, that a compensation be paid to anyone who has suffered damages or loss as a result of breach of these legal obligations.

Normally the objective is to obtain damages (money compensation) or an injunction, prohibition and specific performance (court order). In civil law, for the plaintiff to win a case, he/she needs to show that the claim is correct on the balance of probabilities on the presented evidence and must convince the court of its correctness. Civil law primarily resolves disputes between individuals and organisations through contract and tort law.

Chapter 5

Basic legal concepts

Contract

A contract is a legally enforceable agreement and one of its key elements is that it must be based upon a bargain, i.e. each party must give something in return for the promise given by the other. What each party promises or undertakes to do in the fulfilment of the contract is called *'Consideration'*. A contract is enforceable since there is legal action available in case one party should fail to comply with his promise under the agreement. One of the functions of contract law, for instance, is to provide a means of dispute resolution between parties who have entered into legally enforceable contracts, which is known as contractual relationship, should something goes wrong.

The usual remedy is money compensation, known as damages. When a party does not comply with the terms of a contract, a breach of contract is said to have occurred. An important doctrine of English Law is privity of contract. This states that third parties are unable to sue on a contract that does not concern them.

Rights

A right is some liberty relating to a person that is protected by the law. Example: the possession of property. Where a person exercises a right, s/he does so by virtue of another person owing a duty towards her/him.

Obligation

An obligation exists where parties are in a relationship of right and corresponding duty. A handy example of obligation is a contract in which the parties are under legal duty to perform/fulfil their promise under the agreement.

Liability

A person is under a liability (or is liable) when he owes a duty or an obligation to another. For example, a doctor owes a patient a duty of care and will be liable if he/she breaches that duty of care.

Crime

A crime is an unlawful act or default which is an offence against the public and renders the person guilty of the act liable to legal punishment (e.g. stealing, killing, and attacking someone violently).

Property

Legal 'property' is that which the subject of rights is, e.g. Land and other things that can be owned by a person. Real property is land. Personal property ('chattels') is all other kinds of physical property and also includes contract rights, company shares, patents and copyrights.

Ownership

Ownership is the concept that relates a person to property over which he has exclusive control.

Persons

A person in law is an entity which is capable of having rights and undertaking duties. A thing is the subject of rights and duties. Persons may be either natural or artificial. A natural person is a human being. An artificial person is a corporation created under the law.

Burden of Proof

Under criminal law burden of proof is generally used to describe the threshold that a party seeking to prove a fact in court must reach in order to have that fact legally established. For instance, the burden of proving the defendant's guilt is on the prosecution, and they must establish the fact beyond a reasonable doubt. Criminal law prosecution must demonstrate they are guilty beyond all reasonable doubt and the defendant is always innocent until proven guilty by the prosecution.

Affidavit

Affidavit is a voluntarily sworn declaration of written statement of facts under oath or by affirmation to be true. Affidavits are commonly used to present evidence in court.

Abduction

Abduction means to take a person away by means of persuasion, fraud, or force. Some jurisdictions also require that the abductee, the person abducted, be a child or that the abductor intends to marry or defile the abductee or subject him or her to prostitution or concubine. Parental abduction, a parent's abduction of his or her child, is a crime. Although the terms abduction and kidnapping are, at times, used interchangeably, kidnapping is narrower, generally requiring the threat or use of force.

Abet/Abetment

This simply means to criminally assist another person in the commission of a crime, e.g. in planning a crime, escaping from a crime, or in the actual commission of the crime.

Abscond

To abscond in legal term means to leave a jurisdiction secretly or suddenly, to avoid arrest, or prosecution, or leaving with another person's money or property.

Accomplice

Accomplice means a person who knowingly, voluntarily, or intentionally gives assistance to another in (or in some cases fails to prevent another from) the commission of a crime. An accomplice is criminally liable to the same extent as the principal. An accomplice, unlike an accessory, is typically present when the crime is committed.

Accused

An accused person is someone who has been arrested for or formally charged with a crime.

Acquittal

This means at the end of a criminal trial, a finding by a judge or jury that a defendant is not guilty. An acquittal could sometimes signify that a prosecutor failed to prove his or her case beyond a reasonable doubt, but not that a defendant is innocent.

Actus Reus

A guilty act which does not make a person guilty of an offence unless he has a guilty mind too

Admissible Evidence

It simply means, evidence that is formally presented before the trier of fact (*i.e.*, the judge or jury) to consider in deciding the case. The trial court judge determines whether or not the evidence may be proffered. To be admissible in court, the evidence must be relevant (*i.e.*, material and having probative value) and not outweighed by countervailing considerations (*e.g.*, the evidence is unfairly prejudicial, confusing, a waste of time, privileged, or based on hearsay). This is also termed *competent evidence*; *proper evidence*; *legal evidence*.

Alibi

A defence to a criminal charge alleging that the accused was somewhere other than at the scene of the crime at the time it occurred.

Conspiracy

Conspiracy refers to an agreement between two or more people to commit an illegal act. The act is always committed with intention to achieve the agreement's goal

Contempt of Court

The in or out behaviour of court that violates a court order, or otherwise disrupts or shows disregard for the court. Refusing to answer a proper question, to file court papers on time, to pay court-ordered child support, or to follow local court rules can expose witnesses, lawyers, and litigants to contempt findings. Contempt of court is punishable by fine or imprisonment.

Cross Examination

During a trial, the interrogation of a witness performed by the opposing party in order to inquire further regarding the subject matter of the direct examination or to question the credibility of the witness

Diplomatic Immunity

Diplomatic immunity is a status granted to diplomatic personnel that exempts them from the laws of a foreign jurisdiction.

The Vienna Convention of Diplomatic Relations (1961), which most states have ratified, offers diplomats acting as officials of state almost total protection from subjection to criminal, administrative, and civil laws belonging to the country in which the diplomatic mission is located. Diplomats assigned to missions located in foreign countries remain subject to the laws of their home countries. The diplomat's country of origin has prerogative over whether or not a host country may prosecute a diplomat under its (i.e. 'foreign') laws.

Extradition

Extradition is the removal of a person from a requested state to a requesting state for criminal prosecution or punishment. Put differently, to extradite is to surrender, or obtain surrender of, a fugitive from one jurisdiction to another.

CHAPTER 6

Basic Legal Jargons

Trespass

When there is direct interference with the person or property of another

Libel

Libel is a method of defamation expressed by print, writing, pictures, signs, effigies, or any communication embodied in physical form that is injurious to a person's reputation, exposes a person to public hatred, contempt or ridicule, or injures a person in his/her business or profession.

Manslaughter

Manslaughter is the act of killing another human being in a way that is less culpable than murder. For instance, to kill someone through accident, self-defence yourself, or when you are adequately provoked.

Voluntary manslaughter is intentionally killing another person in the heat of passion and in response to adequate provocation.

Involuntary manslaughter is negligently/accidentally causing the death of another person.

Mens Rea

Mens Rea refers to criminal intent. Moreover, it is the state of mind indicating culpability which is required by statute as an element of a crime.

Penal notice

Directions attached to a court order if breached can result in imprisonment.

Litigation

Legal proceedings

The tort of negligence

Negligence involves a duty of care, and the damage which is suffered as a result of a breach of that duty. To succeed in a claim for negligence, the plaintiff must show that the damage or injury suffered was caused by the defendant's breach of duty.

Treason

The offense of betraying one's own country by attempting to overthrow the government through waging war against the state or materially aiding its enemies

Verdict

Opinion presented by a judge or jury on a question of fact rather than law.

Oath

A verbal statement/ promise by a person of religious belief to tell the truth in a law court. This is traditionally made over the Bible and Quran by Christians and Moslems respectively. Others without faith may use different statements other than oath.

Order in Court

A direction by a judge in court to maintain silence

Plea

A defendant's reply to a court charge

Precedent

The earlier decision in a case which has established principles that can be used as authority for future cases

Exhibit

A document or an item used during court trial. A photograph taken at a crime scene for purposes of evidence in court is a good example of 'exhibit'.

Mitigation

Reasons submitted on behalf of a guilty person in order to excuse or partially excuse the offence committed in order to minimise the sentence. A person guilty of stealing a very expensive drug can mitigate his act by pleading that he committed the crime to save his dying mother as he is jobless and could not afford to buy the drug.

Injunction

Injunction is a court order restraining a person from carrying out a course of action or directing a course of action to be complied with. An injunction can be a court order preventing a media publication which can damage a person's reputation or it can stop a building work being carried out on another person's property.

Defendant

The individual or organisation being sued, and have defend their position during legal proceeding

Litigant

A person/organisation, that brings legal action against another person.

Litigant in Person

A person who chooses to represent themselves in court, without a lawyer

Claimant

A person or an organisation who sues another in legal action

Civil Cases

Civil cases involve breaches of contract, divorce and children, landlords and tenants, employment (unfair dismissal), debt problems, personal injury etc.

Summary judgement

Judgement obtained from the claimant/plaintiff where there is no defence or no valid grounds for defence.

Criminal Cases

Criminal cases include offences against the person or the state. For instance, murder, fraud, theft (stealing, robbery etc.), damage to property, rape, battery, etc.

Advocate

A lawyer representing a person in court

Appeal

An application to Higher Court to review a lower court's decision

Appellant

A person or organisation who appeals

Bail

To discharge or release a suspect/ defendant from custody until s/he appears in court, usually on the grounds of financial security.

The Bar

The collective name for lawyers

The Bench

The collective name for judges

Bench warrant

A court order issued by a judge to arrest a defendant/ offender who was absent in court during proceeding.

Barrister

A lawyer who specialises in advocacy (speaking in court) in England & Wales. In most civil law jurisdiction, there is no division in the legal profession. A lawyer is a barrister or state attorney who practices almost every area of law and does every work for their clients.

Solicitor

Solicitors are lawyers who don't usually represent clients in court but advise them on all legal matters. (Especially in England & wales)

Judiciary

Judiciary is the collective name for judges.

Adjourned

To suspend a court hearing for a short period of time

Witness

A person who gives evidence in court

Recorder

A member of the legal profession who is appointed to act in a senior capacity on a part time basis and waiting to progress to full time judge

Writ:

A writ is written legal document to initiate a legal proceeding/ action.

Notary public:

A notary public is an authorised person to swear oath and execute deeds.

CHAPTER 7

Popular Latin words in Law

CORPUS JURIS:

Body of laws

Contra Perferentem:

Against the party who brought forth an ambiguous term in contract

Contra

Meaning 'Against'

Contra Legem

Against the law

Bona Fide

In good faith/sincerely/genuinely/very honest without any deception

Bona Vacantia

Ownerless goods

Certiorari

A writ seeking judicial review

Certeris Paribus

With other things the same/equal

Inter Alia

Among other things

In Personam

In respect of person/about persons

In Rem: In respect of property

Habeas Corpus

A writ challenging the legality of a detention

Ibid

In the same place

Idem

The same

I.E (i.e.):

ID EST meaning 'that is'

Ex- Gratia

Something done by favour/ voluntarily

Ex- Parte

To reach a decision for one party in the absence of the other in court

Et Cetera: And so on and so forth

Et Al

Among others/ among other things

Dictum/Obiter

An incidental statement made in court by a judge that can be given consideration or a persuasive value.

De jure

Something established in law

De Facto

An established fact considered to be the truth but not legally/officially instituted

Post Mortem

After death

Per Capita:

Strict division of money or resources equally per head

Per Se

Something that is as a matter of law

Non Liquet

A verdict in which positive guilt or innocence cannot be determined

Lex Scripta

Codified or written law

Lingua Franca

A common language spoken by all

Intra Vires

Acting within legal authority/power

Ultra Vires

Acting beyond legal authority/power

Terra Nullius

Land belonging to no one/ no man's land

Supra

Above/Overlord

Subpoena

A writ compelling a witness to testify or produce evidence in court under penalty for failure to do so

Ratio Decidendi

Legal reason/point for a court decision made by a judge

Ratio Scripta:

A written opinion/reason for decision in court

Quasi

Similar to or in resemblance of the original

Quantum

How much something costs

Pro Bono

 A professional legal work done for free, usually for the benefit of the general public

Pro Forma

As a matter of formalities

Sine qua non

'Without which'

Prima Facie

First impression/at first glance/sight

Stare Decisis

Stand by earlier decision.

Status Quo

As it stands or the existing state of affairs